Dedicated to the long suffering masses of Zimbabwe.

"You who are in good positions, you and your wives, today you enjoy many comforts; perhaps a good education, a fine house, good contacts and many missions on which you are delegated which open new horizons to you. But all your wealth forms a hard shell which prevents your seeing the poverty that surrounds you. Take care," Frantz Fanon.

≡ Contents

⋟Acknowledgements.

The following short essays were compiled by the author after reading works of Acemoglu, D & Robinson, Francis Fukuyama and Frantz Fanon. Please see the Bibliography.

Fukuyama and Acemoglu have raised a very serious issue in their writings, that is, nations fail due to extractive institutions. These short essays will help us to understand and view, through the eyes of Fukuyama et.al, the reasons why some countries are poor, in this case Zimbabwe.

Finally, the author has also included Frantz Fanon's lamentations on the poor state of African states after achieving their political independence.

Introduction.

Our country, Zimbabwe is a beautiful country with an amazing resilient people. We have seen the economy of Zimbabwe crumbling down. There are so many reasons to why Zimbabwe has been reduced from being the breadbasket of Africa to a nation of vendors. Zimbabwe needs a real change. Replacing a poorly administered autocracy with an equally incompetent democracy will get us nowhere. It needs a change of leadership with a political mindset different from the one we have seen from the Zanu PF regime.

The suffering we are facing in Zimbabwe is sufficient enough for us to demand for change. There is no doubt that the Mugabe era will finally reach to its end-game. As a country, we have a lot of work to do post Mugabe. Politics of patronage is so much embedded in our politics; it will take an enormous effort to reduce it.

It is up to individuals to describe Mugabe a legend or villain. Some may lament and bemoan the end of pan-africanism; others will celebrate the end of a dictator. Even yesterday, while others were calling Mandela a hero, others were calling him a sell out and traitor. Mugabe is no exception. It is beyond doubt that Mugabe is a man who divides opinion and stimulates so much debate. I will leave that for posterity. It is a time to look ahead and visualize a new Zimbabwe without Mugabe.

Many of us would like to figure out how to transform Zimbabwe, once the "jewel of Africa" to a fully functioning democracy, suitable for the twenty first century and beyond.

We also need to educate our people. A large number of our eligible voters vote for populist policies. Some vote on the basis of personalities rather than policies. Most of our voters do not have the expertise to devote to the careful study of complex public policy issues. New social actors should form a coalition which has no strong stake in the existing corrupt system. The coalition will have to change the rules by which the current system has been operating. A coalition of progressive social groups will eliminate one particular form of clientelism, the ability of political parties to secure support through the distribution of jobs.

In view of Zimbabwe's economic atrophy, the short essays here attempt to address the following questions:

- o What is political development?
- o   What is political decay?
- o What can Zimbabwe do to curb the rampant corruption bedevilling the nation?

- o What are the tough challenges of rebuilding Zimbabwe post Mugabe.
- o Is Zimbabwe a failing state?
- o Is democracy just an expression of ideas?
- o How communist China did broke the mold from poor to rich and what should be the lessons for Zimbabwe?
- o Is Mugabe's main challenge a crisis of legitimacy in the Zanu PF system?

Finally, the last essay is adapted from Frantz Fanon's *The Wretched of the Earth;* who died of leukaemia on *December 6, 1961* at a National Institutes of Health facility in Bethesda, Maryland, USA.

 **ONE:**

Political development is more than the exit of Mugabe from the political arena in Zimbabwe.

Political development is not the exit of Mugabe only from our political arena. It could be a mere microcosmic catalyst that will trigger a new era.

What is political development?

Political development is the underlying rules by which we can organize ourselves. Political development is change over time in political institutions, which is the evolution of the state, rule of law and democratic accountability. Changes in political institutions must be understood in the context of economic growth, social mobilisation, and the power of ideas concerning justice and legitimacy.

Social mobilisation concerns the rise of new social groups over time and changes in the nature of the relationship between and among these groups. Our youth is a new political social group rising today in Zimbabwe. Our youth are conscious of themselves as a people with shared interests or identities. One of the main distinctive features of our youth is that they are a well educated people with no job opportunities in Zimbabwe.

Most of my political associates are the disillusioned, highly educated, displaced and unemployed youth of Zimbabwe scattered in the diaspora. We share a lot of ideas on various social network platforms. One major issue that keeps coming up on our discussions is the issue of good governance. In simple terms, governance is the system or manner of government or the act of governing a country.

The political institutions I am going to focus on in this discussion are the state, rule of law and mechanisms of accountability.

The State:

The state is a hierarchical, centralized organization that holds a monopoly on legitimate force within our borders. To most of us, we want a state which strives to treat citizens on a more impersonal basis, applying laws, recruiting officials, and undertaking policies without favouritism. I was in pain when one South Africa based Zimbabwean youth made this comment, "Zimbabwean youth are fed up of the current system, it's either you know someone or you come from a rich family to make it in life. After attaining our education, our dreams are shattered. The movement to South Africa and Botswana is the order of the day. Zimbabweans are naturally hard workers, but unfortunately all their sweat is being used in other countries and for peanuts."

How true. This is one glaring example showing that the current system in our country is not working. Our state, as an institution is failing the youth and as a result, has failed itself.

The Rule of Law:

We always demand to have the rule of law in Zimbabwe. What exactly do we mean? We have a people made constitution and a judicial system. The rule of law is the second institution I am discussing. One school of thought defines it as a set of rules of behaviour, reflecting a broad consensus within society that is binding on even the most powerful political actors in a society. If a prime minister or president, [including political leaders from opposition parties] changes the law to suit themselves, the rule of law does not exist, even if those laws are applied uniformly to the rest of the society.

To be effective, a rule of law has to be embodied in a separate judicial institution that can act autonomously from the executive. In a nutshell, rule of law must be a constraint on political power. We have to be able to separate rule of law from rule by law. Rule by law represents commands issued by the president but not binding on him.

We need to make sure that the laws will apply impersonally to all Zimbabweans, and that there are no exemptions for a privileged few. Our future government, in new Zimbabwe must be responsive not only to elites and to the needs of those running the government; the government should serve the interests of all citizens of Zimbabwe.

The rule of law is critical for economic development; without clear property rights and contract enforcement, it would be difficult for businesses to break out of small circles of trust. A state that is powerful without serious checks is a dictatorship; one that is weak and checked by a multitude of subordinate political forces is ineffective and often unstable.

Accountability:

The third institution is accountability. Accountability means that the government is responsive to the interests of all citizens – rather than to its narrow self interest. However, in our new Zimbabwe, we need to be very careful when selecting our government. It has to be one that will not change the constitution to prolong its stay in power. Two terms means two terms.

I am mentioning this because we have two types of accountability, which are procedural and substantive accountability. Procedural accountability entails periodic free and fair multi-party elections that allow Zimbabweans to choose and discipline their political leaders.

Substantive accountability means that political leaders will only respond to the interests of the broader society; without necessarily being subject to procedural accountability. This is one way we can end up with tyranny.

However, a school of thought believes that there is a strong connection between procedural and substantive accountability because unconstrained leaders, even if responsive to the common good, usually cannot be trusted to remain that way forever. We have to be wary of the fact that good procedures do not inevitably produce proper substantive results.

I am not so sure whether we will be able to come up with a new government with all three institutions in tandem. We may end up with a new Zimbabwe with a weak state and rule of law but a strong periodic accountability. I am sure most of us would like to see our future president leaving office after two terms.

A new Zimbabwe should have all three sets of political institutions in balance. We have a huge task of educating Zimbabweans post Mugabe. Government officials and civil servants must realise that they are supposed to be servants or custodians of a broader public interest and are legally prohibited from using their offices for private gain. We need to be governed by bureaucracies that are characterised by strict subordination to public purposes, technical expertise, a functional division of labour, and recruitment on the basis of merit.

Our future politicians, unlike the current crop, should not adopt the outward forms of our current state – with bureaucracies, legal systems, elections, etc – and yet in reality rule for private gain.

Favours are being doled to a network of political supporters in exchange for votes or attendance at rallies.

We have to accept that we currently have a weak and ineffective state. Our current government is a very strong despotic power, meaning that its strength is in suppressing journalists and opposition politicians. But is not strong in its ability to exercise infrastructural power, the ability to legitimately make and enforce rules, or to deliver necessary public goods like safety, health and education.

We have struggled to develop high-quality bureaucratic administrations and are mired in high degrees of clientelism (a social order which depends on relations of patronage) and outright corruption.

Surely, replacing a poorly administered autocracy with an equally incompetent democracy will get us nowhere. I have not answered the million dollar question of how to have good governance in new Zimbabwe. This is a question I face every day during my political discourse with my fellow country men and women. This is something we need to debate on. But one cannot begin to understand how a bad government might become good unless one understands what needs to be done.

⧸⧹TWO:

Political Decay

One form of political decay is called repatrimonialization, of which Zimbabwe and many other developing countries suffer from. However, this is also evident in developed countries, but more subtle or covert.

The favouring of family or friends with whom one has exchanged reciprocal favours is a natural form of sociability and is a default manner of human interaction. According to Fukuyama in *The Origins of Political Order*, the most universal form of human political interaction is a patron-client relationship in which a leader exchanges favours in return for support from a group of supporters. Even if new rules are put in place to recruit on the basis of function or talent, there is constant pressure to repatrimonialize the system.

Individuals initially recruited into an institution on impersonal grounds nonetheless often try to pass on their positions to their children or friends. I cannot separate this term from politics of patronage, which is the control of or power to make appointments to government jobs or the power to grant other political favours.

As a country, we have a lot of work to do post Mugabe. Politics of patronage is so much embedded in our politics; it will take an enormous effort to reduce it. To be honest, there are a lot of intelligent and well deserving young turks in the ruling ZANU – PF. Young people who are determined to work with the opposition political parties for the good of the country.

However, due to the fact that Mugabe has resorted to put trust on old, outdated and over recycled guards, repatrimonializing continue to recur. The old guards will continue to appoint their incompetent relatives in our institutions. Our young graduates from universities are left jobless and roaming the streets. This is one sign of political decay taking place.

⫸Three:

Zimbabwe needs a stronger market economy to curb corruption.

Corruption is the scourge of Africa and the Achilles' heel hindering our progress. We have to combat corruption first in order to strengthen our institutions and build a new Zimbabwe. Corruption is a serious impediment to the economic development of our country. Having a strong and effective state involves more than just controlling corruption, but highly corrupt governments usually have big problems in delivering services, enforcing laws, and representing the public interest.

Research has shown that corruption acts as a highly regressive tax. If we set up an anti-corruption commission today, independent from the state and president, we will find that rampant corruption on the part of minor, poorly paid officials exists in today's Zimbabwe, which we already know. But we will find that the vast bulk of misappropriated funds go to elites who are using their positions of power to extract wealth from the population.

Corruption takes many forms, some of them much more damaging to economic growth and political legitimacy than others, so it is necessary for me to now rely on my scholarly literature.

Creation and Extraction of Rents:

For example, a government can place tariffs on imports. The tariffs will strict imports and generate rents [the difference between the cost of keeping a good or service in production and its price] for the government. One of the most widespread forms of corruption around the world lies in customs agencies, where the customs agents will take a bribe in order to either reduce the duties charged or expedite. The ability of governments to generate rents encourages many ambitious people to choose politics rather than entrepreneurship or the private sector as a route to wealth.

However, we must remember that the rents are perfectly legitimate and we cannot completely denounce them. What we can denounce is the abuse of the system. One school of thought has observed that many Asian governments have promoted industrialisation by allowing selected firms to generate excessive profits, provided they plough back into new investment. While we agree that this opens the door to considerable corruption and abuse, it also stimulates rapid growth at a rate possibly higher than market forces on their own would have produced. In the same vein, what has the diamond mining companies in Zimbabwe ploughed back into our community?

Patronage and Clientelism:

These two forms of corruption are the scourge of Zimbabwe and the rest of Africa at large. A patronage relationship is a reciprocal exchange of favours given by the patron to the client in exchange for the client's loyalty and political support.

Clientelism involves mass party organisations distributing widespread favours through complex hierarchical political machines. Clientelism is rampant especially towards general elections. In a new Zimbabwe, we would expect citizens to vote for politicians based on their promises of broad public policies.

Most of our MPs are seen in their constituencies during campaigning and election times only. They will reappear again, unashamedly, towards the end of their term as they seek re-election. During campaigns, our politicians are seen providing individualised benefits only to political supporters in exchange for their votes. Some of the benefits dished out are jobs, cash payments, political favours, agricultural inputs, maize, even cups of sugar.

This undermines good democratic practice. Instead it strengthens existing elites and blocks democratic accountability. In most cases, powerful or wealthy politicians in effect are buying the support of the ordinary citizens. These politicians are interested in promoting their narrow interests. They are interested in promoting the welfare of their clients who provide their base of support but not the public at large. Instead of procuring broad benefits for the poor, clientelistic parties dissipate resources on what are in effect individual bribes for votes.

I am now going to jog your mind. I am going to argue that clientilism is not a form of corruption. Some school of thought has stated that there are a number of reasons why clientelism should be considered an early form of democratic accountability and be distinguished from other types of corruption – or indeed not considered a form of corruption at all.

The first reason is that it is based on a relationship of reciprocity and creates a degree of democratic accountability between the politician and those who vote for him or her. Even though the benefit given is individual rather than programmatic, the politician still needs to deliver something in return for support, and the client is free to vote for someone if the benefit is not forthcoming. Moreover, my scholarly literature argues, clientelism is designed to generate mass political participation at election, something we regard as desirable.

Further, the argument goes on, clientelism should be viewed as an early form of democracy rather than a form of corruption as we see it taking hold in very many young democracies where voting are new and politicians face the problem of how to mobilise voters.

In rural Zimbabwe, where voters are less educated and on no monthly income, it is often easier to get supporters to the polls based on a promise of an individual benefit rather than a broad programmatic agenda. Poor voters can be more easily bought than rich ones, with relatively small individual benefits like a cash gift or a promise of a low-skill job. Zimbabwe politics is a much surer route to wealth for both patrons and clients.

A strong market economy:

However, some schools of thought would argue that clientelism may diminish as countries get richer. They argue that as a stronger market economy develops, the opportunities for privately generated wealth increase, both absolutely and relative to the level of rents that can be extracted by entering politics. For instance, they argue that ambitious young people who want to make large fortunes in the USA do not go into government. They go to Wall Street or corporate America, or start their own companies in places like Silicon Valley. The argument lies in the sense that one who can make money elsewhere will not go into politics for quick riches only. For instance, if I can make a good and decent living out of my profession, trade or business, why would I stoop down for small bribes that could be offered by a clientelistic politician?

Although a stronger economic growth that allows citizens to get richer together is almost impossible and not a total panacea to curb corruption, it is one step forward and will definitely reduce the rampant corruption we witness today. Over the years corruption has perpetuated itself as a cultural habitat. To some, corruption is now a norm. Our challenge in new Zimbabwe is to dismantle this paradigm shift. We can do it if we all work together for a better new Zimbabwe. Zimbabwe should be first before any partisan politics, tribalism or kinship. Our political leaders should abide by the principles of servant leadership and not as a way to get rich quick. You are Zimbabwe, I am Zimbabwe and together we are a nation.

Four:

The tough challenges of rebuilding Zimbabwe post-Mugabe

We are approaching a crossroad; a reality check moment in our entire history in Zimbabwe. There is no doubt that the Mugabe era will finally reach to its end-game. The "I am a war veteran and liberation fighter" mantra will finally get outdated and irrelevant to the younger generation. A new generation of young Zimbabweans will take over control of their motherland. It is up to individuals to describe Mugabe a legend or villain. Some may lament and bemoan the end of pan-africanism; others will celebrate the end of a dictator. Even yesterday, while others were calling Mandela a hero, others were calling him a sell out and traitor. Mugabe is no exception. It is beyond doubt that Mugabe is a man who divides opinion and stimulates so much debate. I will leave that for posterity. It is a time to look ahead and visualize a new Zimbabwe without Mugabe.

Meanwhile, as the circus goes on, we must start to think of the new Zimbabwe we are going to inherit, repair and rebuild post – Mugabe.

The exit of Mugabe is not going to usher in a golden era without our sweating. Things can get worse if we fail to come up with a legitimate leader and a capable government. We will need to work harder and together as a nation. We must start to envisage a sustained economic growth in new Zimbabwe. What do we have to do in order to realise this economic growth? The few prerequisite pointers I am going to discuss here are not exhaustive. A lot more has to be done. It will take many years to repair and rebuild the damage done in the last twenty years, but we can do it.

Having a stable state is a precondition for intensive economic growth. A civil war or interstate conflict has very negative consequences for growth. At all costs, we must avoid civil strife and bloodshed. There is a large literature linking good governance to economic growth. Some school of thought has maintained that good governance is endogenous: it is the product of economic growth rather than a cause of it. For instance, one of the reasons why there is so much corruption in Zimbabwe is that our government is not paying our civil servants adequate salaries to feed their families, so they are inclined to take bribes.

The rule of law is also a prerequisite to economic growth. The key aspects of rule of law that are linked to growth are property rights and contract enforcement. Unfortunately, as in most African states, stable property rights exist only for a certain elites, this is not sufficient enough to produce long term economic growth. The way the land issue was mishandled in Zimbabwe still scares investors, albeit the genuine reasons behind it.

Our judiciary system, which has been adulterated by the current corrupt system, needs cleansing. In fact, the judiciary system should protect the rights of the citizens first. This will promote the rule of law, which in turn will buttress a strong democratic state. The state should not have overwhelming powers to ignore individual property rights. Investors will simply flee. Our judiciary system should be strong enough to keep the state on check and point it to the rule of law book. Some school of thought also believes that there is a strong correlation linking development to democracy. However, the relationship between growth and democracy may not be linear – that is, more growth does not necessarily always produce more democracy. Growth appears to favour stable democracy, the reversal causal connection between democracy and growth is much less clear. In a nutshell, while having a coherent state and reasonably good governance is a condition for growth, it is not clear that democracy plays same positive role.

There has been a large body of democratic theory arguing that modern liberal democracy cannot exist without a vigorous civil society. The mobilization of social groups allows weak individuals to pool their interests and enter the political system; even when social groups do not seek political objectives, voluntary associations have spill over effects in fostering the ability of individuals to work with one another in novel situations – what is termed social capital.

Unfortunately, in our present system, any social group that seeks to pool its resources together is deemed a political threat, even if its members do not seek political objectives. Some rogue elements in Zimbabwe will make sure that any social group seen as a threat to the current status quo is quickly nullified. A good case is the abduction of pro-democracy activist Itai Dzamara, leader of Occupy Africa Unit Square. The group is now in disarray and moribund since the abduction of its charismatic leader.

Fukuyama, in his *The Origins of Political Order* noted that the correlation noted above linking economic growth to stable liberal democracy presumably comes about via the channel of social mobilization: growth entails the emergence of new social actors who then demand representation in a more open political system and press for a democratic transition. When the political system is well institutionalized and can accommodate these new actors, then there is a successful transition to full democracy.

However, as a caution, we must be aware of the fact that, also, a highly developed civil society can also pose dangers for democracy and can even lead to political decay. Groups based on ethnic or racial chauvinism spread intolerance; interest groups can invest effort in zero-sum rent seeking, excessive politicization of economic and social conflicts can paralyse societies and undermine the legitimacy of democratic institutions. The recent utterance by Mugabe that Kalangas are an uneducated lot is quite unfortunate and should be disdained in its strongest terms. It is un-statesmanlike, divisive and ill advised.

Economic growth can also create legitimacy for the government that succeed in fostering it; however, legitimacy also rests on the distribution of the benefits of growth. Growth that goes to a small oligarchy at the top of the society without being broadly shared often mobilizes social groups against the political system. For instance, the revenue from our diamond fields in Zimbabwe does not seem to be benefiting the majority of the poverty stricken villagers in the areas.

Finally, for economic growth to be realized, a country must have a modern political system which consists of a strong state, a rule of law, and accountability. As mentioned above, one day, the circus will pass town, and normalcy will return, leaving us with a lot of work to do.

FIVE:

Is Zimbabwe a failing State?

The research and writing of Fukuyama in his *Origins of Political Order* is an insight. For most of us in developing countries, democracy is a dream. Democracy has been so elusive to such an extent that it is now imaginary. To many of us, we only read or hear that democracy is an all encompassing political institution that is known to have good political and economic institutions. We only hear that it is stable, peaceful, prosperous, inclusive, and has extremely low levels of political corruption. Many of us would like to figure out how to transform Zimbabwe, once the "jewel of Africa" to a fully functioning democracy, suitable for the twenty first century and beyond.

According To Fukuyama, there are a number of problems with this agenda. It does not seem very plausible that extremely poor and chaotic countries could expect to put into place complex institutions in short order, given how long such institutions took to evolve. The struggle to create modern political institutions is so long and painful that people living in industrialised countries now suffer from a historical amnesia regarding how their societies came to that point in the first place.

Most of us can only remember that Zimbabwe was once the bread basket of Africa, and today, it is possibly the first vending nation in the world. Everyone has to vend in order to survive.

27

Still, after Mugabe, the struggle to create a modern functioning state is going to be long. The sordid failings of the Mugabe regime will come into a full glare after his departure, together with his whole entourage. The failings we are currently seeing are just a tip of the iceberg.

In the first place, how did we come to have a state? Our ancient ancestors lived in tribal societies. They owed primary obligation not to a state but to kinfolk, they settled disputes not through courts but through a system of retributive justice. How come we still have retributive justice in today's Zimbabwe? Today, as I am writing, a pro-democracy activist, Itai Dzamara, calling for Mugabe to step down, was abducted by yet unknown men in broad day light. We have not heard anything from the so-called state of his whereabouts. A functioning state should have, at least, come up with an explanation of what took place on the day of his abduction. Someone applied the barbaric, ancient and uncivilized retributive justice.

A state is the centralized source of authority that holds an effective monopoly of military power over a defined piece of territory. Peace is kept by the state's army and police, a standing force that can also defend the community against neighbouring tribes and states.

Today, Zimbabwe is not in a state to defend her-self from other invading states. This is a country which has dismally failed to run its own airline, let alone owning a fleet of high tech war-jets.

Many countries have been and are still investing in high tech warfare hardware. For instance, a happy trigger American soldier, operating from any of the American military bases situated in Botswana, seated on an armchair can cause so much damage to Zimbabwe by the use of drones.

Fukuyama further pens that in time; our ancestors formalised as written laws rather than customs or informal traditions. These formal rules were used to organize the way that power was distributed in the system, regardless of the individuals who exercised power at any given time. Institutions, in other words, replaced individual leaders. Those legal systems were eventually accorded supreme authority over society, an authority that was seen to be superior to that of rulers who temporarily happened to command the state's armed forces and bureaucracy. This came to be known as the rule of law.

Is there the rule of law in Zimbabwe? No. The moment one uses retributive justice on his fellow countrymen, and the state fails to intervene and justify, there is no upholding of the rule of law. The moment state security agencies override decisions made by the judiciary, there is no upholding of the rule of law. The moment a President manipulates the country's constitution to prolong his rule; there is no upholding of the rule of law. The moment political party cronies ignore property rights of individuals; there is no upholding of the rule of law. The moment a political heavy weight allows vendors to sell vegetables and fruits along street pavements in the Central Business District, therefore bypassing the council bylaws, there is no upholding of the rule of law. The moment the judiciary system is politicised, corrupted and adulterated by the ruling elite, there is no upholding of the rule of law.

Finally, Fukuyama noted that certain societies not only limited the power of their states by forcing rulers to comply with written law: they also held them accountable to parliaments, assemblies, and other bodies representing a broader proportion of the population. Some degree of accountability was present in many traditional monarchies, but it was usually the product of informal consultation with a small body of elite advisers. Modern democracy was born when rulers acceded to formal rules limiting their power and subordinating their sovereignty to the will of the larger population as expressed through free and fair elections.

Alas, how many of us, through the ballot box and an adulterated electoral system stands a chance to limit the power of our leaders. In a nutshell, for a successful modern liberal democracy, the three pre-requisite ingredients; which is the rule of law, accountable government and a functioning state, are missing in Zimbabwe.

When these institutions cannot protect our interest, then that government must go. When corrupt, greedy elites and cronies – most often rich and powerful, entrench themselves over time and begin demanding privileges from the state, then, that government must go.

To conclude, I will note that Fukuyama stated that a successful modern liberal democracy combines all three sets of institutions in a stable balance. The fact that there are countries capable of achieving this balance constitutes the miracle of modern politics. The state, after all, concentrates and uses power, to bring about compliance with its laws on the part of its citizens and to defend itself against other states and threats. The rule of law, an accountable government, on the other hand, limits the state's power according to certain public and transparent rules, and then by ensuring that it is subordinate to the will of the people.

SIX:

Is democracy just an expression of ideas?

Zimbabwe government is now facing a significant challenge as young, educated and out of employment youth begin to demand a share of political power. Will this lead to the eventual appearance of formal democratic accountability in Zimbabwe? This question has prompted me to ask the following questions. Why is democracy more established in some societies than others?

Why democracy has become a global phenomenon in the twentieth century? One school of thought stated that democracy has taken hold as a result of the underlying idea of democracy and ideas clearly propagate rapidly across international borders via social media, internet, radio and television.

Still, to an inquisitive mind, why do the ideas of human equality or democracy take off in some periods and not others? I would like to refute the notion that liberal democracy does not represent a universal trend but something culturally specific to Western civilisation. Then, further to a more inquisitive mind, why this particular idea arose in the West and not elsewhere?

One school of thought answered this by stating that democracy is not the expression of an idea or a set of cultural values but as the by-product of deep structural forces within societies. Meanwhile, social scientists have long noted that there is a correlation between high levels of economic development and stable democracy. Well, does this explain the fact that most of the world's rich industrialised countries are democracies? Can we accept that most authoritarian countries are much less developed?

Another school of thought has argued that while countries may transition from authoritarian to democratic government at any level of development, they are much more likely to remain democracies if they rise above a certain threshold of per capita income. Going back to Southern African, let's look at the disparities between Zimbabwe and Botswana? Botswana's economy is far much stronger when compared to its neighbour, Zimbabwe. Can we, therefore deduce that Botswana is more democratic than Zimbabwe? The economy of South Africa is undoubtedly one of the strongest in Africa. Therefore, can one be correct if they postulate that by virtue of having a stronger economy; South Africa will always be more democratic than Zimbabwe?

What is the connection between economic development and democracy? One school of thought suggests that economic growth affects democratic institutions via social mobilisation. It is believed that the key concept is the division of labour. The division of labour is limited by the size of the market. As markets expand through increased trade in both commercial and industrial economy a new division of labour would arise and deepen. This division of labour will entail the creation of new social groups. These new groups, once excluded from participation in the political institutions, would demand a share of political power and therefore increase pressures for democracy.

My concern with new social groups is their vulnerability to corruption. They can easily get bought off by the rich, corrupt and already seasoned politicians to support at most very limited democracy.

However, a stable democratic system will emerge only if these newly mobilized groups are successfully incorporated into the system and allowed to participate politically. Instability and disorder will occur if these groups do not have institutionalised channels of participation.

The idea of democracy is within the mindset of the pro-democratic forces of Zimbabwe. Why has this idea failed to gain traction? Is this due to the fact that the bulk of ZANU-PF supporters are rural peasants with a low social mobility?

Remember I have already stated somewhere that democracy is an idea. I will start by highlighting an argument raised in 1861 by a thinker called Mill in his treatise *Thoughts on Parliamentary Government*. He argued that "the assembly which votes the taxes, either general or local, should be elected exclusively by those who pay something towards the taxes imposed." Mill believed that it was better to impose direct tax to all citizens. That would remind them of their obligations to be vigilant about how the government spend their money. He further contested one man one vote.

He argued that if it is asserted that all persons ought to be equal in every description of right recognised by society, "not until all are equal in worth as human beings." What he meant is that different classes of people should have different numbers of votes based on their level of education: an unskilled labour one vote; a foreman, three; and a lawyer, physician or clergyman five or six. He noted that Louis Napoleon had just been elected president of France by millions of "peasants who could neither read nor write, and whose knowledge of public men, even by name, was limited to oral tradition." In a nutshell, he meant that uneducated people should not vote as they do not exercise the franchise responsibly.

Unfortunately, this kind of conservative thinking may end up getting abused and we could see ethnic minorities getting disenfranchised. It has happened before in history. This would be wrong. Governments should be accountable to citizens, and that all citizens capable of exercising good political judgement.

However, the above assertion has prompted me to question the seriousness of our voters. Do they ever consider the level headedness and competency of their MPs before casting a vote on their names? Is it high time to call for all of our MPs to hold at least a higher education qualification and pledge to be guided by a code of conduct? The calibre of some of our MPs is a disgrace and dishonour to the nation. Our voters should think twice before casting their vote.

Unfortunately, some of our educated politicians have let us down as well and the above argument will not hold much water. Some conservative thinkers have also argued that it is pointless to open up franchise since true democracy is impossible to achieve. They argued that the different regime types made little difference to actual life because all were in the end controlled by elites. The "political class" maintains itself in power under a wide variety of institutions and will simply use democratic ones to do the same. Democratic procedures like regular elections and press freedoms do not guarantee that the people will be adequately represented.

Echoes of these nineteenth century conservative arguments remain contemporary in political landscape. A large number of our voters vote for populist policies. Some vote on the basis of personalities rather than policies. Most of our voters do not have the expertise to devote to the careful study of complex public policy issues.

Some policies are put forward for a referendum before implementation. To some extent, the result is not the accurate representation of popular will. The best-organised and most richly resourced group or party usually dominate. Subtle political intimidation is also used in order to coerce voters.

How can we achieve democracy when voters are irresponsible and easily intimidated? How can we have democracy when we vote for populist views, care less about pragmatic and developmental policies? How can we achieve democracy when we vote for the most decadent and incompetent MPs? How can we have democracy when our corrupt politicians control state institutions and maintain their status quo?

Are we caught in a vicious circle? Our economy is in a quagmire, meaning it cannot support democracy. As stated above, democracy requires a strong economy to flourish. How will our economy get strong when our political leaders and elite plunder state coffers and care less about the welfare of the state? How can we get out of this vicious circle when our all powerful political leaders turn to the army, police and unorthodox ways to silence us? Therefore, is democracy just an expression of ideas?

≋SEVEN:

How China broke the mold from poor to rich: A lesson for Zimbabwe?

China and Zimbabwe are comparative authoritarian and excessive bureaucratic comrades; both with a streak of dictatorial stranglehold on their citizens. In 1949, China had a highly extractive economy. In 2015, Zimbabwe has got a highly extractive economy. The Chinese Communist Party dominated the political arena. Zanu PF is still dominating Zimbabwe politics since 1980, and a lot of opposition party obituaries. Just like Mugabe in Zimbabwe, Mao dominated the Communist Party and the government. Mao nationalized land and industry. He abolished all kinds of property rights. As with all extractive institutions, Mao's regime was attempting to extract resources from the vast country he was now controlling. The Chinese Communist Party had a monopoly over the sale of produce, such as rice and grain, which was used to heavily tax farmers. Mao claimed that in fifteen years, China would catch up with British steel production, yet, there was no feasible way of meeting these targets.

To meet the plan's goals, scrap metal had to be found, and people would have to melt down their pots and pans and even agricultural implements such as hoes and plows. Workers who ought to have been tending the fields were making steel by destroying their plows, and thus their future ability to feed themselves and the country. The result was a calamitous famine in the Chinese countryside.

In Zimbabwe, on October 2013, Zanu PF, through its economic blue print ZimAsset, claimed that it is going to create 1.5 million jobs by 2018. The Vision of the Plan is "Towards an Empowered Society and a Growing Economy". The execution of this plan will be guided by the following mission: "To provide an enabling environment for sustainable economic empowerment and social transformation to the people of Zimbabwe" [ZimAsset.pg 9]. Today, the ZimAsset is reduced to a mere decorative document as Zimbabwe's economy is crumbling down. The state is reduced to a nation of vendors.

However, in China, one Deng Xiaoping argued, "No matter whether the cat is black or white, if it catches mice, it's a good cat." It did not matter whether policies appeared communist or not; China needed policies that would encourage production so that it could feed its people. Deng was soon to suffer for his new found practicality. Mao announced that the regime was under threat from "bourgeois" interests that were undermining China's communist society and wishing to recreate capitalism.

Mao's announcement strikes a chord with the speech given by the President of Zimbabwe, Robert Mugabe in September 2013, when he berated the United States and former colonial power

Britain and its allies for trying to control his nation and its resources, telling them to remove their "illegal and filthy sanctions." "Shame, shame, shame to the United States of America. Shame, shame, shame to Britain and its allies," "Zimbabwe is for Zimbabweans, so are its resources. Please remove your illegal and filthy sanctions from my peaceful country. We paid the ultimate price for it and we are determined never to relinquish our sovereignty and remain master of our destiny. Zimbabwe will never be a colony again."

In China, Mao responded to Deng's argument by introducing the Cultural Revolution. The Cultural Revolution was an attempt by Mao to reassert his beliefs in China. Soon the Cultural Revolution would start wrecking both the economy and many human lives. Units of Red Guards were formed across the country: young, enthusiastic members of the Communist Party who were used to purge opponents of the regime. Many people were killed, arrested, or sent into internal exile.

Again in Zimbabwe, we are reminded of the so called "Green Bombers". This was a national youth service programme, whose graduates were derogatorily dubbed the "Green Bombers" because of the colour of their uniforms. It was launched by the late Youth minister Border Gezi in 2001 to "transform and empower youths for nation building through life skills training and leadership development".

The programme was, however, discontinued due to lack of funding and after recruits had been widely accused by opposition parties of inciting political violence especially during election time. The government was accused of conscripting desperate and unemployed youths into its controversial national youth service and brainwashing them to become blind and violent zealots of the ruling Zanu PF party.

However, Mao retorted to concerns about the extent of violence, stating, "This man Hitler was even more ferocious. The more ferocious, the better, don't you think? The more people you kill, the more revolutionary you are." Similarly, President Mugabe once retorted, "I am still the Hitler of the time. This Hitler has only one objective: justice for his people, sovereignty for his people, recognition of the independence of his people and their rights over their resources. If that is Hitler, then let me be Hitler tenfold. Ten times, that is what we stand for."

China only managed to turn around its ailing economy after Mao's death. I am not insinuating that we, in Zimbabwe, cannot turn around our economy with Mugabe in power. However, it would be difficult to do so because the extractive economic and political institutions he has presided over are still in existence. We need to restructure them and make them inclusive. We need political and economic reforms.

With Mao gone, there was a true power vacuum in China, which resulted in a struggle between those with different visions and different beliefs about the consequences of change. Even after Mugabe, many Zanu PF stalwarts will not abolish the extractive institutions they had created. They are part of the same group of people brought to power by the Zanu PF revolution. The Gamatox and the Zvipfukuto faction groups in Zanu PF are culprits; both had presided over the current economic and political institutions bedevilling our economy today. Today's China has maintained its extractive bureaucratic political institutions inherited from Mao.

However, in China, Deng found himself in power after intra-political struggles. Deng did not want to abolish the communist regime and replace it with inclusive markets. He thought that significant economic growth could be achieved without endangering their political control: they had a model of growth under extractive political institutions that would not threaten their power, because the Chinese people were in dire need of improved living standards and because all meaningful opposition to the Communist Party had been obliterated during Mao's reign and Cultural Revolution.

To achieve this, they had to repudiate not just the Cultural Revolution but also much of the Maoist institutional legacy. They realized that economic growth would be possible only with significant moves toward inclusive economic institutions.

At the Twelfth Nations Congress in September 1985, Deng achieved an almost complete reshuffling of the party leadership and senior cadres. In came much younger, reform minded people. Deng and his new reformists launched a series of further changes in economic institutions. The rural economy took off first with the introduction of incentives, which led to a dramatic increase in agricultural productivity. In the urban economy, state enterprises were given more autonomy, and fourteen "open cities" were identified and given the ability to attract foreign investment. Market incentives in agriculture and industry, then followed by foreign investment and technology set China on a path to rapid economic growth.

China's Achilles heel would be her inability to completely abandon her extractive political institutions. For instance, one Chinese dissident commented that in today's China, "Big companies can get involved in huge projects. But when private companies do so, especially in competition with the state, then trouble comes from every corners [sic]." Growth under extractive political institutions is quite unfavourable to foreign investment. The Communist party in China controls the media, including the Internet.

Some school of thought has noted that China has achieved economic growth not thanks to its extractive political institutions, but despite them: its successful growth experience over the last three decades is due to a radical shift away from extractive economic institutions and toward significantly more inclusive economic institutions, which was made more difficult,

43

not easier, by the presence of highly authoritarian, extractive political institutions.

In August 2015, President Robert Mugabe signed into law the Reserve Bank of Zimbabwe (RBZ) debt assumption bill. The development means government has taken over the central bank's $1.2 billion debt which includes some $200 million given out as agro-support to top officials in the ruling party. It also means that Zanu PF top chefs who benefited from the farm mechanisation equipment supplied by the RBZ never paid for it. The bill was passed in parliament despite the spirited objection from opposition MPs. This is a clear case of an extractive economic institution benefitting the Zanu PF elite. In fact, shuffling a debt from one extractive institution to another will not alleviate the problem.

The suffering we are facing in Zimbabwe is sufficient enough for us to demand for change. History is not destiny. Extractive institutions can be replaced by inclusive ones. But it is neither automatic nor easy. A confluence of factors, in particular a critical juncture coupled with a broad coalition of those pushing for reform or other propitious existing institutions, is often necessary for a nation to make strides towards more inclusive institutions.

We cannot continue to have extractive economic institutions, which are synergistically linked to extractive political institutions, which concentrate power in the hands of a few Zanu PF cronies.

China managed to break the mold from poor to rich. We can do it in Zimbabwe. However, if we, Zimbabweans, cannot remove Zanu PF, we must push it to make political reforms first.

⊳EIGHT:

Mugabe's main challenge is a crisis of legitimacy in the Zanu PF system.

The critical weakness that will eventually topple Mugabe is a failure of legitimacy. In political science, legitimacy is the popular acceptance of an authority, usually a governing law or regime. A political regime is legitimate when its participants have certain beliefs or faith in regard to it: "the basis of every system of authority, and correspondingly of every kind of willingness to obey, is a belief, a belief by virtue of which persons exercising authority are lent prestige" (Weber 1964: 382).

Weber distinguishes among three main sources of legitimacy—understood as both the acceptance of authority and of the need to obey its commands. People may have faith in a particular political or social order because it has been there for a long time (tradition), because they have faith in the rulers (charisma), or because they trust its legality—specifically the rationality of the rule of law (Weber 1990 [1918];

Legitimacy is not justice or right in an absolute sense; it is a relative concept that exists in people's subjective perception. All regimes that are capable of effective action must be based on some principles of legitimacy. Some political economists believe that there is no such thing as a dictator who rules purely by force. A tyrant can rule his children, old men, or perhaps his wife by force, if he is physically stronger than they are, but he is not likely to rule more than two or three people in this fashion and certainly not a nation of millions.

When the opposition in Zimbabwe say that Mugabe is ruling them by force, what they mean is that Mugabe's supporters', including Zanu PF, the Central Intelligence Organisation and other state agents are able to physically intimidate them. But what made these supporters loyal to Mugabe? Certainly not his ability to intimidate them physically: ultimately it rest upon their belief in his legitimacy authority.

Security apparatuses can themselves be controlled by intimidation, but at some point in the system, Mugabe has loyal subordinates who believe in his legitimate authority. It is not always the case that a regime needs to establish legitimate authority for the greater part of its population in order to survive.

Already we can see the cracks from the likes of expunged and now squealing Didymus Mutasa. Mutasa was the Zanu PF Secretary for Administration before his expulsion for allegedly supporting the presidential ambitions of former Vice President Joice Mujuru. He reminds me of Squealer in George Orwell's *Animal Farm*. Every tyrant has his sycophants, and Napoleon had one in Squealer, a clever pig who (as the animals say) "could turn black into white."

We now get the confirmation from Mutasa that Robert Mugabe lost to Morgan Tsvangirai in the 2008 elections. A larger part of the population knew that Mugabe had lost, but Zanu PF dug its heels, knowing that it had the legitimacy from the securocrats and army generals.

A lack of legitimacy among the population as a whole does not spell a crisis of legitimacy for Zanu PF unless it begins to infect the elites tied to the revolutionary party itself, and particularly those that hold the monopoly of coercive power. The threat to Mugabe is the top Zanu PF brass, the armed forces and the police. When we speak of a crisis of legitimacy in the Zanu PF system, we are speaking of a crisis within the top elite whose cohesion is essential for Mugabe to act.

Where does Mugabe's legitimacy spring from? It could be from personal loyalty on the part of a pampered top brass or those who still believe in his ideology. His land re-distribution programme, has not gone unnoticed, albeit the devastating economic consequences that ensued.

The more we see purges going on in Zanu PF, the more Mugabe is losing his legitimacy. President Mugabe has been around long enough to suffer an internal crisis of legitimacy.

Some observers have labelled Zimbabweans as being too passive, fatalistic or endlessly melancholy. One thing these observers prefer to ignore is the fact that Mugabe is old and could have retired some time back. However, he cannot do so as long as the few thousand elites, powerful securocrats want him to stay put. They still see his legitimacy in power, for various reasons best known to them. Some of the reasons are quite obvious. Some of the Mugabe's close cabal have been enriching themselves by looting state resources. They are happy for the old man to stay at the helm, as long as they can keep their ill gotten riches. The moment these elites decide that enough is enough, Mugabe will not last.

Like so many called "strong man" of Africa, Mugabe will have to admit that he will eventually have to confront the fact that he has no long term legitimacy, and no good formula for solving the long term economic and political problems we now face.

Finally, revolutionary parties or one party rule tend to degenerate over time, and to degenerate more quickly when faced with a well educated, agitated and technologically advanced jobless youth. President Mugabe is a charismatic character. Revolutionary regimes may govern effectively in their early years by virtue of charismatic authority. However, with Zimbabwe facing a poor service delivery from the government, high rate of unemployment, lack of accountability, a dying industry, the legitimacy of the nonagenarian is always fading by the day. We shall hear more and more squealing from the revolutionary party.

≥NINE:

To avoid chaos, Mugabe should facilitate a peaceful political transition in Zimbabwe before his departure.

Political transition is the process or a period of change from one state or condition to another. Political reform is a change in governance aimed to bring improvement. Zimbabwe needs a peaceful political reform, based on the formation of a coalition of social groups interested in having an efficient, incorrupt government. Underlying the formation of such a coalition is the process of socioeconomic modernisation.

As it is, these new social actors should form a coalition which has no strong stake in the existing corrupt system. In other words, social mobilisation, driven by economic modernisation will create conditions for the elimination of patronage and clientilism [a social order which depends on relations of patronage]. In the long term, we will also curb corruption.

The coalition will have to change the rules by which the current system has been operating. A coalition of progressive social groups will eliminate one particular form of clientelism, the ability of political parties to secure support through the distribution of jobs.

What should President Mugabe of Zimbabwe do in order to avoid a bloody transition after his departure from the political arena? The president should facilitate a peaceful political transition while in office. This should be done in the most transparent and democratic way possible.

My fear is that time when Mugabe leaves office either through natural causes or retirement. We may go through a short period of chaos, if not a bloody political transition, until, like a phoenix arising from the ashes – a national leader emerges. The future leader of Zimbabwe could be someone out of the leadership picture at this juncture, especially if social groups work together and select a capable leader from their various multi-party groups.

However, looking at the Zimbabwe scenario and the political stranglehold President Mugabe holds over the country, it would be premature to talk of political reform before a peaceful political transition. Why? Currently, any coalition in Zimbabwe will struggle to make headway, especially when faced with brutal state machinery and an uneven electoral field; hence my argument that President Mugabe is a key ingredient to a successful political transition, followed with political reform.

This view is also supported by Samuel Huntington in *Political Order in Changing Societies* – that societies need order before they need democracy, and that they are better off making an authoritarian transition to a fully modernised political and economic system rather than jumping directly into democracy.

Some of my readers here may argue that what is the point of putting off democratisation, in favour of a ruthless and/or corrupt and incompetent government. After all, reform requires dislodging the current corrupt and incompetent political actors. Instead, I urge we work around the corrupt and incompetent system and organise new social forces that will benefit from the creation of a cleaner and more capable form of government. We will have a peaceful transition if we follow such a sequence. Of course, the coalition will face resistance from the current crop of politicians as they are the ones benefitting from the status quo. At the same time, we cannot have a smooth and peaceful transition without involving one of the key political players.

President Mugabe is part of the solution. He is a key player in our politics and it is a fact. He has to allow a free and fair election in 2018. To avoid chaos after his departure, he should facilitate the selection of new leader, presumably from within his own party. The new heir apparent will face the coalition in free and fair elections. If beaten in the elections, his political party should concede defeat and allow the winner to form the next government. This strategy will also afford Mugabe his overdue exit from the political arena.

Meanwhile, a coalition of social groups should form a strong opposition and start working towards engagement of all stakeholders, gearing for transition and finally transformation. It would be interesting to have a coalition of social groups interested in having an efficient and incorrupt government. However, the opposition political parties should learn to work together. It is possible to imagine civil society groups and opposition political leaders organising reformist coalitions that press for public-sector reforms, an end to gross corruption and the implementation of a free and fair 2018 election. Meanwhile, the prolonged stay of President Mugabe at the helm of Zimbabwe politics is holding back any political, social or economic progress.

≥TEN:

The poignant failures of the Zanu PF cabal and Mugabe's betrayal of the masses.

The opinions expressed in this article are Frantz Fanon's, who died of leukaemia on *December 6, 1961* at a National Institutes of Health facility in Bethesda, Maryland, USA. His body was returned to Tunisia, where it was subsequently transported across the border and buried in the soil of the Algerian nation for which he fought so single-mindedly during the last five years of his life.

The Zanu PF cabal should have known the pitfalls in front of it when we achieved our political independence in 1980. I cannot describe these pitfalls better than one Frantz Fanon in his book "The Wretched of the Earth". In this article, I will make sure I will not bastardise Frantz's beautiful prose and thoughts by attempting to scribe my own. I will give it as it is. However, I am going to introduce some fictitious characters; which are the Zanu PF cabal, Robert Mugabe, the masses and Zimbabwe.

Some readers who will find the views in this article absurd are described by Frantz as suffering from cognitive dissonance. He said, "Sometimes people hold a core belief that is very strong. When they are presented with evidence that works against that belief, the new evidence cannot be accepted. It would create a feeling that is extremely uncomfortable, called cognitive dissonance. And because it is so important to protect the core belief, they will rationalize, ignore and even deny anything that doesn't fit in with the core belief."

The Zanu PF cabal which took over power at the end of the colonial regime was an underdeveloped party. It had no practically economic power. Neither financiers nor industrial magnates were to be found in this party. The objective of the Zanu PF cabal as from attaining independence was to mobilise the people with slogans of independence and to leave the rest for future events. When the Zanu PF cabal was questioned on the economic programme of the newly independent Zimbabwe, their replies could not have been realistic, for they were completely ignorant of the economy of the country they were just inheriting. The economy of Rhodesia [Zimbabwe, before independence] has always developed outside the limits of their knowledge.

Zanu PF had nothing more than an approximate bookish acquaintance with the actual and potential resources of the new Zimbabwe's soil and mineral deposits; and therefore they could only speak of these resources on a general and abstract plane.

The dearth of economic knowledge forced Zanu PF into an artisan economy. From its point of view, which is inevitably a very limited one, a national economy is an economy based on what may be called local products. Since Zanu PF found it impossible to open up new factories that would be more profit earning both for them-selves and for the country as a whole, they surrounded civil servants with chauvinistic tenderness in keeping with the new awareness of national dignity.

Since 1980, the national economy of Zimbabwe never set on a new footing. It was concerned with the maize and ground nuts harvests. There has never been any change in the marketing of basic products, with no industries being set up in the country. Zimbabwe continued, for a while, to be European's small farmers who specialise in unfinished products. Zimbabwe continues to export raw materials.

The Zanu PF cabal demands nationalisation of the economy. To the cabal, nationalisation quite simply means the transfer into native hands of those unfair advantages which are a legacy of the colonial period. The Zanu PF cabal insists that all the big foreign companies should pass through its hands; and by so doing it has discovered its historic mission: that of intermediary.

As soon as the land was nationalised, through manifold scheming practices, the Zanu PF cabal managed to make a clean sweep of the farms expropriated from the white farmers, thus reinforcing their hold on the land. But they did not try to introduce new agricultural methods, nor to farm more intensively, nor to integrate their farming systems into a genuinely national economy.

In fact, the Zanu PF elite, including the war veterans, insisted that the state should give or fund them a hundred times more facilities and privileges than enjoyed by the poor peasants, who eke a living in the infertile and exhausted ancestral soils designated to the natives by the white supremacist Ian Smith, Prime Minster of Rhodesia and his predecessors.

When the white owned farms were expropriated, the exploitation of agricultural workers intensified and made legitimate. Using two or three slogans, these new farmers, will demand an enormous amount of work from the agricultural labourers, in the name of the national effort of course. There is no modernisation of agriculture, no planning for development and no initiative. The new Zanu PF farmers demands solid investments and quick returns.

The Zanu PF cabal does not hesitate to invest in foreign banks the profit that it makes out of its native soil. On the other hand large sums are spent on display; on cars, mansions, and numerous mistresses, popularly known as small houses.

Zanu PF's mission is not to transform the nation; but to effectively be the transmission line between the nation and capitalism, rampant though camouflaged, which today puts on the mask of neo-colonialism. But this lucrative role, this cheap-jack's function, this meanness of outlook and this absence of all ambition symbolizes Zanu PF's incapability. Zimbabwe still exports her precious unpolished diamonds, effectively creating employment for the Western countries.

The spirit of indulgence is dominant at the core of Zanu PF leadership; and this is because, despite their rhetoric, they identify themselves with the British upper class, from whom they took over. The Zanu PF elite is greatly helped on its way towards decadence by the Western bourgeoisies, who visits Zimbabwe's tourists attractions for the amazing flora and fauna, especially big game hunting.

The masses of unemployed Zanu PF youth and supporters for their part line up behind the nationalist attitude; but in all justice let it be said, only follow in the steps of their leaders. From nationalism, the Zanu PF has passed to ultra-nationalism, to chauvinism, to racism and finally to tribalism.

For, in fact, everywhere that the Zanu PF cabal has failed to break through to the people as a whole, to enlighten them, and to consider all problems in the first place with regard to them – a failure due to Zanu PF's attitude of mistrust and to the haziness of its political tenets – everywhere where the Zanu PF cabal has shown itself incapable of extending its vision of the world sufficiently, we observe a falling back towards old tribal attitudes, and, furious and sick at heart, we perceive that race and tribal feeling in its most exacerbated form is triumphing.

Now, that the Zanu PF cabal, since it is strung up to defend its immediate interests, and sees no further than the end of its nose, reveals itself incapable of building up the nation on a stable and productive economy. The revolutionary party which forced colonialism to withdraw is cracking up, and wasting the victory it gained.

Since the Zanu PF cabal has not the economic means to ensure its domination and to throw a few crumbs to the rest of the masses; since, moreover, it is preoccupied with filling its pockets as rapidly as possible but also as prosaically as possible, Zimbabwe sinks all the more deeply into stagnation. And in order to hide this stagnation and to mask this regression, to reassure itself and to give itself something to boast about, the Zanu PF cabal is finding nothing better to do than to give long lectures to the poor masses of the history of the liberation struggle.

As it does not share its profits with the people, and in no way allows them to enjoy any of the dues that are paid to it by the big foreign companies, the cabal discovered the need for a popular leader to whom will fall the dual role of stabilizing the regime and of perpetuating the domination of the party. The Zanu PF cabal draws its strength from the existence of its leader President Robert Mugabe. Mugabe stands for moral power in whose shelter the thin and poverty stricken bootlickers of the nation decide to get rich.

The people who for years on end have seen Mugabe and heard him speak, who from a distance in a kind of dream have followed his contests with the colonial power - Britain, spontaneously put their trust in this patriot. Soon after independence, Mugabe generally embodied the aspirations of the people for independence, political liberty and national dignity. But as soon as independence was declared, far from embodying in concrete from the needs of the people in what touches bread, land and the restoration of the country to the sacred hands of the people, Mugabe has gradually become a caricature of himself. The Zanu PF cronies and elites are happy to prop him in power, for to them, he is like a general president of that company of profiteers impatient for their returns.

Today, Mugabe's contact with the poor masses is so unreal and it is easy for him to believe that his authority is hated and that the services he has rendered his country are being called in question. Mugabe will judge the ingratitude of the masses harshly, and every day that passes will range him a little more resolutely on the side of the state looters. He therefore knowingly becomes the aider and abettor of the state looters who are plunging into the mire of corruption and pleasure.

The economic channels of Zimbabwe are sinking back inevitably into the pre-colonial lines. The national economy, formerly protected, is today literally controlled. The budget is balanced through loans and gifts, while every three or four months the chief ministers or else their governmental delegations go to the erstwhile colonial masters, fishing for capital.

The Zimbabwean people are stagnating deplorably in unbearable poverty; slowly awakening to the unutterable treason of their leaders. This awakening is all the more acute in that the Zanu PF cabal is incapable of learning its lessons. The distribution of wealth that it effects is not spread from out between a great many sectors; it is not ranged among different levels, nor does it set up a hierarchy of half-tones.

The scandalous enrichment, speedy and pitiless, of the Zanu PF cabal is accompanied by a decisive awakening on the part of the people, and a growing awareness that promises stormy days to come.

The Zanu PF cabal annexes for its own profit all the wealth of the country. The poverty of the people, the immediate money-making of the Zanu PF cabal, and its widespread scorn for the rest of the Zimbabweans has hardened thought and action.

But such threats are increasingly leading to the reaffirmation of authority and the appearance of dictatorship. Mugabe, who has behind a lifetime of political action and devoted patriotism, now constitutes a screen between the people and the rapacious Zanu PF cabal since he stands surety for the ventures of that caste and closes his eyes to their insolence, their mediocrity and their fundamental immorality.

Mugabe acts as a braking-power, on the awakening power, on the awakening consciousness of the people. He aides the Zanu PF cronies and hides his manoeuvres from the people, thus becoming the most eager worker in the task of mystifying and bewildering the masses.

Every time he speaks to the people he calls to mind his often heroic life, the struggles he has led in the name of the people and the victories in their name he has achieved, thereby intimating clearly to the masses that they ought to go on putting their confidence in him. Behind him are the Youth League, The Women's League and his Cabinet, who proclaim that the vocation of the people is to obey, to go on obeying and to be obedient till the end of time.

Mugabe pacifies the people. For years on end after independence, incapable on urging people to a concentrate task, unable really to open the future to them or of flinging them into the path of national reconstruction, that is to say, of their own reconstruction; we have seen him reassessing the history of independence and recalling the sacred unity of the struggle for liberation.

Mugabe, because he refuses to break up the parasitic Zanu PF cronies, asks the people to fall back into the past and become drunk on the remembrance of the epoch that led up to independence. He brings the people to a halt and persists in either expelling them from history or prevent them from taking root in it.

During the struggle for liberation, Mugabe awakened the people and promised them a forward march, heroic and unmitigated. Today, he uses every means to put them to sleep, and three or four times a year asks them to remember the colonial period and to look on the long way they have come since then.

Now, the peasants who are scratching out a living in the rural areas; and the unemployed who never finds employment are hungry. They are now sulking and turning away from this nation which they have been given no place.

From time to time, Mugabe makes an effort; he speaks on national events, radio and makes a tour of the country to pacify the people, to calm them and bemuse them. Mugabe is all the more necessary in that there is no party. Zanu PF has disintegrated; nothing is left but the shell of the party, the name - ZANU PF, the emblem - jongwe/cockrel and the motto - Unity, Peace and Development.

The original Zanu PF party, which made possible the free exchange of ideas in its early days, has been transformed into a trade union of individual interests. Today, the party's mission is to deliver to the people the instructions which issue from the summit. There no longer exists the fruitful give-and-take from the bottom to the top and from the top to the bottom which creates and guarantees democracy.

The Zanu PF cabal is sinking into an extraordinary lethargy. The war veterans are only called upon when so-called popular manifestations are afoot, or international conferences or independence celebrations. Today, Zanu PF, the skeleton of its former self, only serves to immobilize the people. The party, which during the early days had drawn to itself the whole nation, is falling to pieces. Zanu PF has become the means of private advancement.

The progressive transformation of the Zanu PF cabal into an information service is the indication that the government holds itself more and more on the defensive. Today there exists inside the Zanu PF cabal, however, equality in the acquisition of wealth and in monopolization. Some have a double source of income and demonstrate that they are specialised in opportunism. The privileges are multiplying and corruption triumphing, while morality declines. The vultures are too numerous and too voracious in proportion to the lean spoils of the national wealth. The party is helping the government to hold the people down. It is becoming more and more clearly anti-democratic, an implement of coercion.

It is the intellectuals of the country, cowed to silence and reduced to political spectators, commentators and analysts to write, "You who are in good positions, you and your wives, today you enjoy many comforts; perhaps a good education, a fine house, good contacts and many missions on which you are delegated which open new horizons to you. But all your wealth forms a hard shell which prevents your seeing the poverty that surrounds you. Take care".

The religious will reiterate the call by saying: If there is no room in your heart for consideration towards those who are beneath you, there will be no room for you in God's house.

The Zanu PF cabal does not worry at all about such indictment. The enormous profits derived from the exploitation of the people are exported to foreign countries. The Zanu PF cabal know that their present fortunate situation will not last indefinitely and they intend to make the most of it. Such exploitation and such contempt for the state, inevitably is going to rise to discontent among the masses of the people.

The Zanu PF cabal must not only be opposed because it is threatening to slow down the total harmonious development of Zimbabwe. It must simply be stoutly opposed because, literally, it is good for nothing. This Zanu PF party, which has turned its back more and more on the people as a whole cannot even succeed in extracting spectacular concessions from the international community, such as investments which would be of value for Zimbabwe's economy or the setting up of certain industries.

Closing the road to the Zanu PF cabal is, certainly, the means whereby the vicissitudes bedevilling Zimbabwe may be avoided, and with them the decline of morals, the installing of corruption within the country, economic regression, and the immediate disaster of an anti-democratic regime depending on force and intimidation. But it is also the only means towards progress.

We have seen time and time again that the Zanu PF cabal never stops repeating that the direction of affairs in Zimbabwe is better under the authoritarian rule of Robert Mugabe. With this in view the party is given the task of supervising the masses, not in order to make sure that they really participate in the business of governing the nation, but in order to remind them constantly that the government expects from them obedience and discipline.

The Zanu PF cabal, which of its own proclaims that it is a national party, and which claims to speak in the name of the totality of the people; secretly, sometimes even openly, organises an authentic ethnical dictatorship.

There should never be a situation whereby the ministers, the members of the cabinet, the ambassadors and local commissioners are chosen from the same ethnological group as Mugabe, or directly from his own family. Such regimes of the family sort seem to go back to the old laws of inbreeding, and not anger but shame should be felt when we are faced with such stupidity, such imposture, such intellectual and spiritual poverty.

We may understand the panic caused in governmental circles each time dear Mugabe falls ill; the Zanu PF cabal is obsessed by the question of who is to succeed him. What will happen to the country if the leader disappears? The Zanu PF cabal which has abdicated in favour of the leader, irresponsible, oblivious of everything and essentially preoccupied with the pleasures of their everyday life, their cocktail parties, their journeys paid for by government money, the profits they make out of various schemes – from time to time these state vultures discover the spiritual waste land at the heart of the nation.

The Zanu PF cabal is a tool in the hands of the government. A political party is not, and ought never to be, the only political bureau where all members of the government and the chief dignitaries of the regime meet freely together. Over the years, the government bigwigs and Zanu PF party officials have grouped themselves around Mugabe. The government services have swelled to huge proportions, not because they are developing and specializing, but because new found cousins and fresh militants are looking for jobs and hope to edge themselves into the already bloated government.

The time for more national crisis is not far off. There are still honest intellectuals in and out of Zimbabwe. They have got no precise idea of politics, but instinctively distrust dishonest. We must know how to use these men and women in the decisive battle that we mean to engage upon which will lead to a healthier outlook for new Zimbabwe.

In conclusion, the government, to be national, ought to govern by the people and for the people. No leader, however valuable he may be, can substitute himself for the popular will; and the government, before concerning itself about international prestige, ought first to give back the dignity to all citizens.

The masses should not have that core belief instilled in them by the Zanu PF cabal, that is, there is no life outside the Zanu PF system. That would be cognitive dissonance. Zimbabwe has not worked well for most of us. More of the same won't work. The change we desire in new Zimbabwe will never be successful if it's from the Zanu PF cabal to the masses. Change should be from the masses to the top. We now need to build a strong new social movement to bring about real change. We must base our policies on justice, freedom, solidarity and equality for all. We need a working economy, which works for all, rejects corruption and opportunism and the plundering of our natural resources; benefiting a few.

We need something different – a new kind of politics: a fairer, kinder Zimbabwe based on innovation, decent jobs and decent public services. We need protection from work and a strong collective bargaining to stamp out workplace injustice. We have got so much to rebuild in Zimbabwe. Everything that everyone will say and does should be about unity, not division. One force. One new Zimbabwe.

Now, a democratic collective action is needed to secure a better Zimbabwe. Our government should never be the property of a president and his cronies. Believe me, real change is possible, unless one is suffering from cognitive dissonance.

Bibliography.

- Acemoglu, D & Robinson, J., Why Nations Fail: The Origins of Power, Prosperity and Poverty. Profile books, London 2012.

- Fanon, F., The Wretched of the Earth. Penguin classics, France 1961.

- Fukuyama, F., Political Order and Political Decay. Profile books, London 2014.

- Fukuyama, F., State Building: Governance and World in the Twenty-First Century. Profile books, London, 2004.

- Fukuyama, F., The End of History and the Last Man. Penguin classics, USA 1992.

- Fukuyama, F., The Origins of Political Order. Profile books, London 2011.